# Buddhism for Beginners

*All you need to start your journey*

Copyright © 2017 by Richard Johnson.

All rights reserved.

# Table of Contents

Introduction
A Brief History of Buddhism
The Spread of Buddhism
The Servant or the Master: Which One are You?
Self-Identification with the Mind and Body
Meditation
The Presence of Mindfulness
The Principle of Karma
Dualistic versus Non-Dualistic Perspectives
The Principle of Non-Substantiality
One's Life and the Environment
Sentient and Non-Sentient Beings
Attachment
The Ten Worlds
Conclusion

# Introduction

There is a famous Buddhist parable called the *Jewel in the Robe*. In this parable, a homeless man wanders the countryside as he looks to eke out a living. He spends his time begging on the streets for food and money.

One day, a rich man is driving through the streets and sees the man sitting on the side of the road. The rich man notices that he is struggling and offers him a ride. As the rich man drives, he gets to know the poor man and invites him to spend the night at his house. The poor man accepts the generous invitation and soon finds himself being able to wash up, eat a warm meal, and sleep in a comfortable bed.

As the poor man lies sleeping, the rich man sneaks into his bedroom and finds the poor man's robe. He has a precious jewel in his hand, which he hides in the lining of the robe. With the valuable jewel securely placed in the robe, he returns it to the room. The next morning, the poor man thanks the rich man for his kindness and continues his journey.

Many years have passed when the rich man encounters the poor man again, sitting on the side of the road. It is clear to the rich man that the poor man is no better off than when he first encountered him.

He asks the poor man why is it that he is still struggling when he has such a precious jewel in his possession. The poor man then feels the lump in the robe's lining. In disbelief, he realizes that he has struggled all this time while possessing a fortune that was beyond his wildest dreams.

Through symbolism, parables help us make connections with ideas that that may be too abstract for us to understand. In this parable, the poor man symbolizes each one of us. The rich man signifies a profound teaching, such as Buddhism. As for the jewel, it represents our most essential nature.

Just like the poor man, we all face struggles in life. We struggle because we are unaware of the precious jewel that lies within us. There is, however, one important difference between the parable and our lives. In the parable, the rich man placed the jewel in the poor man's robe. The jewel that is found within us is not placed there. Rather, it is an inherent aspect of us. It is our most fundamental nature.

All of humanity's suffering, both at the individual and collective level, is due to us being unable to perceive our precious jewel. The purpose of Buddhism is to guide us to the discovery of that jewel. And the purpose of this book is to give the reader a basic understanding of Buddhism and how to make it applicable in his or her daily life.

Before we go any further into this book, I wish to first address some important points for the benefit of you, the reader. First, Buddhism offers a profound perspective on how life works—it goes beyond being a religion. You can benefit from learning about Buddhist principles, regardless of your spiritual beliefs. Rather than imposing dogma of belief systems, Buddhism invites us to journey within and experience its principles for ourselves. For this reason, Buddhism is more like an internal science. It is up to you to determine its validity.

# Chapter One
# A Brief History of Buddhism

*"Whatever precious jewel there is in the heavenly worlds, there is nothing comparable to one who is Awakened."*

—The Buddha

Buddhism has its beginnings in 480 BCE, in Nepal. That was the date when Shakyamuni Gautama, the son Suddhodana, was born. Suddhodana was a chief of a warrior clan and lived a life of royalty. Suddhodana and his wife did not want Shakyamuni to experience the poverty, war, and other societal ills that were common outside of the palace. Out of this concern, the prince was kept from venturing outside the palace walls.

When Shakyamuni turned 29-years old, he received a higher calling; he wanted to develop a deeper understanding of life. He left the palace, leaving behind his wife, his newborn son, and his parents. He ventured out into the community and saw a world that was foreign to him. Unlike the luxurious lifestyle that he was accustomed to, the world outside the palace walls was harsh and unforgiving. He saw people who were stricken with disease, people who were old and feeble, and he saw the corpses of those who passed away. All of these experiences ignited something inside Shakyamuni. He made it his mission to discover the cause of suffering.

In his search for this answer, Shakyamuni encountered many spiritual teachers and became a student of their teachings. Most of the teachers that he met were of the ascetic tradition, meaning that they renounced material comforts and led a life of self-discipline. And so, the man who was born into royalty would choose to live many years in the harshest of conditions. He disregarded all material goods, consumed just enough food and water to stay alive, and exposed his nearly naked body to extreme weather. After years of this punishing existence, Shakyamuni was no closer to discovering the cause of suffering. He left his teachers and continued his pursuit on his own.

Shakyamuni gradually nursed his body back to health and traveled to India. He sat under a Bodhi tree and committed to himself that he would not move from the tree until he received his answer to the cause of suffering. Shakyamuni meditated until he found his answer. When he woke from his meditation, the people of India called him the Buddha, which means the "awakened one." For the remainder of his life, Shakyamuni traveled around India to share his teachings with others.

To be awake is to be enlightened. Shakyamuni was an ordinary human being—he was not a god. However, his awakening would eventually lead to the development of one of the great religions of the world and make him a historic figure.

So, what did the Buddha learn about suffering? Our minds create suffering. It is with this focus that this book was written. This book aims to give those who are unfamiliar with Buddhism an opportunity to explore some of the core principles of Buddhist philosophy and make them applicable to your daily life.

# Chapter Two
# The Spread of Buddhism

*"Hatred is never appeased by hatred in this world. By non-hatred alone is hatred appeased. This is a law eternal."*

—The Buddha

After the death of Shakyamuni Buddha, his followers spread his teachings beyond India. Buddhism made its way into China, Japan, Asia, and eventually, the Western world. As Buddhism migrated across the world, it would develop into different lineages, each with its own interpretation of the original teachings. The following are just a few of the more well-known lineages:

## Theravada Buddhism

Theravada Buddhism is one of the oldest schools of Buddhism. It has a monastic tradition and is orthodox in its teachings, which emphasizes meditation, ethical conduct, and the development of insight and wisdom.

## Mahayana Buddhism

Mahayana Buddhism is less monastic than Theravada, and it places greater attention on rituals. Its teachings are more adaptable to differences in cultures and the changing of the times. For example, it is just as acceptable to sit in a chair while meditating as it is to sit on the floor. In the Mahayana tradition, it is believed that every sentient being possesses an enlightened nature within them. Additionally, the pursuit of enlightenment must involve the working for the happiness of others.

## Tibetan Buddhism

Tibetan Buddhism is one of the more recent lineages of Buddhist schools. It has spread widely from its origins in Tibet and has become well known in the West. The Dalai Lama belongs to this Buddhist school. Its rituals include the offerings of food, meditation, prayer, and chanting.

## Japanese Buddhism

The different forms of Japanese Buddhism originated from China. Two of the commonly known forms of Japanese Buddhism is Zen Buddhism and Nichiren Buddhism. Zen Buddhism has few, if any, rituals. Practitioners use meditation to break through the barriers of the mind that prevent the experiencing of expanded awareness, known as *Satori*. Nichiren Buddhism is commonly practiced in the West and has organizations in most parts of the world. Practitioners of this kind of Buddhism chant to a mandala image, known as the Dai-Gohonzon, which symbolizes the enlightened nature that exists within the life of all sentient beings.

## Is Buddhism a Religion?

Though Buddhism is commonly referred to as a religion, it has many characteristics that make it stand out from most traditional religions. Buddhism does not believe in an external deity that governs our lives. It lacks dogma, and it embraces both the spiritual and the secular. Further, Buddhism does not have a creation story in teachings. Buddhism teachings do not speak of the past or future; rather, its teachings provide a profound perspective on how life works, and how we can live in harmony with it. For all of these reasons, Buddhism is more a lifestyle as well as an internal science for understanding life. I use the description "internal science" because Buddhism involves introspection through a systematic approach, rather than focusing on the external world as traditional science does.

# Chapter Three

# The Servant or the Master: Which One are You?

*"I will not look at another's bowl intent on finding fault: a training to be observed."*

—The Buddha

There was once a servant who worked for his master from a very young age. Now an adult, the servant was becoming frustrated. For most of his life, the servant obediently followed his master's orders. Now, however, the servant had reached a point where he realized that serving his master was causing him much unhappiness. His master was never satisfied with anything that he did. Nothing was ever good enough for his master; he always wanted more and more. Whenever the servant thought that he had performed his job well, his master would criticize him, express doubts, or judge him. Many times his master would build him up with words of praise, only to knock him down with his verbal jabs.

There was one other strange thing about the relationship that he had with his master: he never laid eyes on him. His master stayed in his room and would never venture out. All communication between servant and master was conducted through the master's locked door.

One day, the servant decided that he needed to discuss his frustration with his master. The servant gathered his nerves and boldly went to his master's room. He knocked on the door, but there was no answer. The servant knocked a second time. Still, there was no answer. The servant started to feel concerned. Perhaps something had happened to his master. He reached for the doorknob and realized that the door was unlocked. Never before had his master's door been unlocked. Out of concern, the servant did the unthinkable: he opened the door.

The servant stood there in disbelief. The room was empty. There was no furniture, no rugs, no wall hangings, and no master. The servant came to a shocking realization that the master he had been serving all his life did not exist.

This parable of the servant and his master is to point to the relationship that most of us have with our minds. The servant symbolizes us while the master represents our minds. Like the servant, most of us live out our lives according to the orders that are given by our minds. Our lives are often filled with thoughts of what we did wrong, what we should fear, who we should be angry with, or why we are not good enough.

Buddhism refers to the mind as a "monkey mind." Like a monkey, it is always chattering at us. The reason why we listen to our minds is that we have personalized our thoughts. In other words, we believe that the thoughts that we think reflect who we are as an individual. A person who considers themselves to be intelligent is because of all the knowledge that they have acquired. A person who is shy believes this because of the thoughts that they have of themselves. They may have thoughts like "I am not good enough," or "I should not draw attention to myself." How we see ourselves is a result of the thoughts that we hold of ourselves. Similarly, we judge others by the thoughts that we have of them.

The Buddha's purpose was to find a way to end suffering. Because we identify with our thoughts, we suffer. The Buddha transcended his mind through the powerful tool of meditation. When we transcend the mind, we no longer identify with it. Transcending the mind does not mean we no longer have thoughts; rather, we change our relationship with them. The mind may continue to chatter away, but we no longer get involved with it. Because we do not get involved with the mind's chatter, our minds become quiet. Here is a simple exercise to demonstrate to yourself that you are not your thoughts:

1. Close your eyes and take a few moments to relax.

2. Now imagine a full moon. Try to make the image as real as you can.

3. Now imagine a rose, again make it as real as you can make it.

4. Lastly, imagine a black cat. Make the image as vivid as possible.

Now open your eyes. Did you learn something from this exercise? You imagined a full moon, a rose, and a black cat. These objects were created through your thoughts, but at no time did you mistake yourself for any of the items. This exercise demonstrates to you that you are not your thoughts.

The reason why you define yourself by some of the thoughts that you experience is that you have given them the focus of your attention. No thought has its own power. It is us who give thoughts their power by making them important to us. In fact, there is no experience that you will ever have that has an inherent meaning to it. Just as we give power to our thoughts, we give meaning to our experiences. This is why Buddhism states that all suffering arises from the mind. Buddhism can teach us how to change our relationship with our minds. Instead of us being the servant of the mind, we can become the master.

# Chapter Four

# Self-Identification with the Mind and Body

*"Let none find fault with others; let none see the omissions and commissions of others. But let one see one's own acts, done and undone."*

—The Buddha

Are you aware of your thoughts? Are you aware of the sensations of your body? Are you aware of your perceptions? If you answered "yes" to all these questions, then who are you? If you are aware of all these things, then you cannot be them. Most of us base our sense of identity on our minds and bodies. If we are worried, worry permeates our entire being. If we are sad, our being becomes sadness. If we are in love, that is what we experience.

Because we identify ourselves with our minds and bodies, we experience ourselves as a separate self, which is why you do not confuse your sense of self with this eBook for example. Because you identify yourself with your mind and physical body, you cannot be something outside of your body. But this an illusion as well. During deep sleep, you have no sense of self or experience. In deep sleep, you experience pure consciousness, unlike during REM sleep when you experience dreams. As mentioned before, your essential being is awareness.

# Exercise #1

1. Find a quiet place to sit that is comfortable. You can sit either on the floor or a chair.
2. Close your eyes and allow yourself to relax by placing your attention on the flow of your breath. Keep your awareness on your breath as you inhale by focusing on the sensations in your nose, throat, and chest during inhalation. Do the same thing during exhalation by experiencing the sensations as your breath travels out of your body. Breathe naturally as it is important that you make no effort at any time during this meditation. An alternative to following your breath is to observe the rising and falling of your abdomen.
3. As you breathe, you will experience thoughts, perceptions, and sensations; they will have different qualities to them. Some will be pleasant while others may be uncomfortable or even frightening. Regardless of what you experience, do not interfere with them. Do not try to control, change, or analyze them. Be like a scientist who is committed only to observing them.
4. As you observe, be aware that you are the one that is observing these mental functions. You

are the one who is observing thought, sensation, and perception; thus, you cannot be these things. Try to find the one that is doing the observing. Keep in mind that anything that you can detect with your awareness cannot be the one that is doing the observing, for it is also observed.

# Chapter Five

# Meditation

*"Resolutely train yourself to attain peace."*

—The Buddha

In the previous exercise, you hopefully felt, even if only for a brief moment, what it is like to experience life free of conceptual thinking.

The mind is conceptual, that is how it functions. The mind transforms the information that we receive through our five senses. Whenever we take in information from the environment through perception, touch, hearing, hearing, or taste, the mind conceptualizes that information. The mind is unable to comprehend information that is not phenomenal. Anything that we can experience is considered phenomenal, while anything that cannot be detected by our senses is non-phenomenal. This is why we identify with our minds. Buddhism uses meditation to transcend the mind to observe the mind's functions as well as experience life with greater clarity. The following is a meditation that can help you begin to create space between you and your mind.

Note : It is recommended that you first review this exercise and other meditations in this book before performing them as they contain a lot of information.

Another alternative is to read them out loud while recording and then play them back when you are ready to meditate.

## Exercise #2

1. Find a quiet, comfortable place to sit. You can sit either on the floor or a chair.
2. Close your eyes and allow yourself to relax by placing your attention on the flow of your breath. Keep your awareness on your breath as you inhale by focusing on the sensations of your breath during inhalation. Do the same thing during exhalation by experiencing the sensations as your breath leaves your body.
3. Breathe naturally as it is important that you make no effort at any time during this meditation.
4. An alternative to following your breath is to observe the rising and falling of your abdomen.
5. As you breathe, you will experience thoughts, perceptions, sensations, and sounds. Some will be pleasant while others may be. Regardless of what you experience, do not interfere with them. Do not try to control, change, or analyze them. Like in the previous exercise, commit only to observing them.
6. Notice how all that you experience is transitory, impermanent. Your thoughts,

perceptions, and sensations will appear and then dissolve.
7. Notice that you are aware of all these mental functions; however, they are not you. You are not your thoughts, perceptions, or your sensations.
8. Place your awareness on a thought that you are experiencing. Observe without judgment or trying to control it. Observe the thought until it fades away. Can you detect where it went?
9. Now place your attention on a thought that is appearing in your awareness. Can you detect where it arose from?
10. Now track a thought with your awareness until it fades away. Before the next thought arises, what do you experience?
11. The space between your thoughts may seem like black, empty space. Place your attention on this space. As you practice this meditation, you will be able to increase the time you spend in this space. This space indicates that you have transcended the conceptual mind; you have moved beyond thought. This is the space from which all mental phenomena arise. With practice, you can access this space anytime you wish. This is your portal to your Buddha nature.

# Chapter Six

# The Presence of Mindfulness

*"Drop by drop is the water pot filled. Likewise, the wise man, gathering it little by little, fills himself with good."*

—The Buddha

What prevents us from achieving higher states of consciousness is our self-identification with the mind and body. By personalizing our thoughts, our perceptions, and sensations, we believe that we are our thoughts, perceptions, and sensations. Since these mental functions are constantly changing, our experience of ourselves is constantly changing.

When we develop greater awareness, we realize that we are not the functions of the mind and body; instead, we are the one that observes these functions happening. With this understanding, we lose our identification with our experiences in life. Your essential nature is never touched or colored by that which you experience. An example of this would be if we shined a beam of light on ice or a fire. The light illuminates the ice and fire, but it is not affected by the cold of the snow or the heat of the fire. Our essential nature is consciousness, and consciousness is aware of experience but is not affected by it.

We experience ourselves as the mind and body because we have devoted our attention to them. Because we pay attention to our thoughts, they become energized. When our thoughts become energized, they become our reality. We are unable to experience our deeper selves because thought is stealing our attention from it. Here is an example:

Frank wakes up in the morning and gets ready for work. Even before getting out of bed, he is thinking about his agenda for the day, about what he needs to do when he arrives at work. While taking a shower, Frank thinks about the emotional conversation he had with his girlfriend the other day. He also thinks about the fact that he still needs to select a gift for his parents' anniversary. Frank gets into his car and drives to work, all the time thinking of how much he would like to take time off to go camping. Frank arrives at work, and for the entire day, he thinks about the next meeting, the phone calls that he needs to return, and the decisions he needs to make. At the end of the day, Frank sits down and watches a movie. Though he is enjoying the movie, his mind intermittently drifts off as he thinks about the issues that are concerning him. He continues to think about these things when he retires to bed, only to cease his thinking when he finally falls asleep.

Frank represents the vast majority of humanity in that he lives his life through the time machine known as thought. Most of our thoughts have to do with the past (which we call memory) or the future (which we call anticipation). It is these two thoughts that consume most of our lives at the expense of being present or mindful. When we experience the past or the future, we are unable to experience the present, which does not get caught up in time. From a Buddhist perspective, time is just another illusion of the mind as there is only the present moment.

So what is the present moment? It is awareness. Awareness is the only constant. Thoughts, perceptions, sensations, and experiences are always changing; however, awareness is non-changing. In order words, you are the present moment. You are presence, not as your mind or physical body, but as your awareness. The following is a simple mindfulness meditation.

## Exercise #3

1. Find a place that is comfortable for you. It can be indoors or outdoors.
2. Sit down and allow yourself to relax. For the next ten minutes, take notice of what is happening within you (i.e., thoughts, emotions, sensations, or feelings) and around you. Whatever you notice, do not judge, evaluate, or analyze it. You are to just to be aware of it.
3. If you can go longer than ten minutes, allow yourself to do so if you desire. Practice this each day, increasing the length of your observation each time.

4. When doing this exercise, you should stay relaxed. You cannot get this exercise wrong. Even if you catch yourself making a judgment, allow yourself to experience this so-called mistake without judgment.

# Chapter Seven

# The Principle of Karma

*"When watching after yourself, you watch after others. When watching after others, you watch after yourself."*

—The Buddha

Most of us are familiar with the Buddhist teaching called karma. The principle of karma, however, is widely misunderstood. One misunderstanding is to attribute karma when negative events happen to us. Someone may have a streak of bad luck and believe that it was caused by their karma. Another misunderstanding is that it is difficult to change one's karma, and that it takes a lifetime of spiritual practice. In fact, the powers to be in India reinforced these misunderstandings of karma among those belonging to the lower caste. By embracing this belief, the lower caste accepted their position in society, which is useful when it comes to government maintaining control of this population.

The truth of karma is liberating and allows us to take control of our destiny, regardless of where we may find ourselves today. Karma has three components: desire, action, and memory. These three components create the karmic cycle. The following is an example of how the karmic cycle works:

Imagine a person walking through town and passing a bakery. The smell of freshly baked pastries fills the air. This smell causes the person to recall a memory of the last time he or she ate pastries. The memory elicits the desire to taste pastries again. In response to the desire, the person walks into the bakery and purchases the pastries. The eating of the pastries reinforces the old memory and will lead to desire for pastries in the future. By taking action to fulfill their desire, this person has provided energy for their karmic cycle to complete itself.

Now let us look at the same scenario with a slight twist to it. The person is walking down the sidewalk, smells the pastries, and experiences the desire to eat them, but this time he or she reacts differently. Instead of purchasing the pastries, the person passes by the bakery and visits the park, where he or she takes time to relax and enjoy the peace of their surroundings. By taking a different form of action, this person has changed the karmic cycle. The person has created a new memory, which will lead to new desires in the future.

We change our karma every time we react differently to our experiences in life. Our old karma ends whenever we take on a new form of action. With this understanding, we can develop a greater clarity to the true meaning of karma. Karma is not about what happens to us; it is about how we react to life. When we learn to be consciously aware of how we react to life, we can choose how we want to respond. By making a conscious decision as to how we respond in any given situation, we have taken an important step to becoming the master of our minds.

# Chapter Eight

# Dualistic versus Non-Dualistic Perspectives

*"See them, floundering in their sense of mine, like fish in the puddles of a dried-up stream—and, seeing this, live with no mine, not forming attachment to experiences."*

—The Buddha

In Western culture, we have been socialized into developing a dualistic perspective, and this perspective creates our experience of life. The word "dual" means consisting of two parts, and the word "perspective" refers to how we perceive things. Our dualistic perspective shows up in every aspect of our lives, particularly in our thinking and in our language. Here are some examples:
- "Good or bad."
- "Up or down."
- "Right or wrong."
- "Either/or."
- "Happy or sad."
- "Inside and outside."
- "Life and death."
- "Us and them."
- "Mine and yours."

In Western society, we do not even think twice when expressing this kind of thinking as it seems so natural to us. As an example, take the concept "lost and found." We can get lost when we are driving to a destination, or we can "find" ourselves by asking for directions or using a map. Our experience of being lost can be drastically different from being found. When we are lost, we may feel frustrated or even fearful, while we may feel a sense of relief when we find our way again.

The same is true with the concept of "mine and yours." This dualistic perspective may also directly impact our experience of the moment and is often unquestionably accepted by us. The concept of "mine and yours" is born from a sense of scarcity and is a function of the ego. There are indigenous cultures that do not have a concept of "mine and yours" or "lost and found." Because of this, their experience of life is vastly different than ours.

From the non-dual perspective, life is not divided between good and bad, mine and yours, or right and wrong. From the non-dual perspective, there is no one truth for how things should be, for truth is subjective and is based on perspective. Going back to the previous examples, getting lost and claiming possessions as being ours makes sense from the perspective of our society. For some indigenous people, the idea of getting lost does not make sense. For them, home is where ever they find themselves. Similarly, the concept of "this is mine and this is yours" does not make sense because they believe in sharing everything that they have. In their culture, these perspectives are their truths.

Having a non-dual perspective leads to a life of less judgment and greater tolerance, inclusion, acceptance, and sense of connection with all that we experience. Our relationships are enhanced because we do not focus on the differences between us.

One way to start experiencing a non-dual perspective is to start training yourself to experience life without attaching concepts to it. The following exercise is a good way to start.

## Exercise #4

1. Sit down and make yourself comfortable.
2. Close your eyes and focus on your breath, allow yourself to become relaxed.
3. Now open your eyes and look around at your surroundings. What is the quality of your experience as you view your environment? You may wish to rate your experience from 1-10 with 10 being the highest.
4. Close your eyes again and allow yourself to relax. I want you to imagine that you are an alien from another planet and that you have been sent down to Earth to observe what it is like here. You do not know about this planet, you have no words to describe your what you see, and you have no concepts for what you experience. All you have is your immediate, direct experience.
5. Keeping all of this mind, open your eyes and observe your surroundings again. You can

scan your entire environment or focus on a particular object that you find interesting, or you can do both. Take your time and observe.
6. When you are ready, rate your experience of observing without the use of concepts. Was there a difference from the first time? What were those differences?
7. If you could not detect a difference, that is okay. Continue to practice this technique until you can detect a difference in the quality of your experience when observing.

## Chapter Nine

# The Principle of Non-Substantiality

*"'All conditioned things are impermanent'—when one sees this with wisdom, one turns away from suffering."*

—The Buddha

The Buddhist principle of non-substantiality, also known as emptiness, may seem abstract. Understanding it leads to developing a new perspective toward life that is most profound.

Have you ever wondered where things come from? When I say "where things come from," I mean the very essence from which every thing arises. Where do trees come from? A common response would be from a seed. Where did the seed come from?

We logically conclude that the seed comes from the tree. When viewed from this conventional perspective, we find ourselves caught in the age-old chicken and the egg dilemma of which came first. What would your response be if you were asked the same question of a rock or a star? Where do rocks come from? Where do stars come from? A scientist may tell you that stars are created when clouds of hydrogen, helium, and dust combine together and then contract, that this contracted combination forms stars. Igneous rocks are created when magma, under pressure from the earth, solidify. The next logical question would be where do hydrogen and helium come from? Where does magma come from? Where does the Earth, that creates pressure on the magma, come from?

Because of our dualistic perspective, scientists are researching the answers to these questions by searching for their answers in the phenomenal world. The word "phenomenal" refers to those things that we can perceive through our five senses. Rocks, stars, trees, chickens, and eggs are all phenomenal because they can be detected by one or more of our five senses. But what if the answer to the chicken and egg riddle is that neither one was first? What if both the chicken and egg arise from the non-phenomenal? The word non-phenomenal refers to that which is undetectable to our five senses. In fact, it cannot be conceptualized by the mind.

According to Buddhism, the answer to where all phenomenal objects arise from, including us, is *Ku*. Given that the nature of Ku is non-phenomenal, it cannot be conceptualized. Buddhist use meditation to gain an understanding of Ku. For the purpose of this book, Ku can be defined as the ultimate reality, and its characteristics include oneness, being eternal, and infinite in its potential to express itself.

From the level of the intellect, we can better understand Ku by comparing it to quantum physics. Using a rock as an example, a rock is made of elements such as iron, aluminum, oxygen, and silicon. Going deeper into the rock, we can ask what the individual elements are made of. The answer to that would be atoms. Traditional scientific theory viewed atoms as being solid; they were the smallest unit of matter. Our theories of physics were turned upside down with the advent of quantum physic. Quantum physics demonstrated that the atom is not solid. Atoms are made of subatomic particles which are separated by vast distances of space. Further, these subatomic particles themselves are not solid either; they are created out of fluctuations in energy. The essence of the rock is formless. It is from this formlessness, which contains energy and information, from which everything we know manifests. Ku is just like this.

Here is a simple meditation that you can use to develop a greater understanding of Ku, beyond just reading about it.

# Exercise #5

1. Sit down in a comfortable position and close your eyes.
2. Breathing normally, focus your attention on your breath by placing your awareness on the sensations that you experience during inhalation and exhalation.
3. Take on an attitude of complete allowing and acceptance for whatever you experience.
4. Observe the perceptions, thoughts, sensations, feelings, and emotions that arise within you. Allow them to come and go on their own

accord. All you need to do is be the observer of them.

5. Now place your attention on your thoughts. Observe your thoughts as they appear and fade in the space of your awareness. Remain as the observer. Do not judge, evaluate, or analyze your thoughts, allow them to be just as they are. Simply be aware of them.
6. You may find yourself experiencing racing thoughts. If so, acknowledge that your thoughts are racing.
7. Do not judge your experience should you have disturbing thoughts; your thoughts have no power other than that which you give them. Let your thoughts move about your consciousness freely. Allow yourself to stay as the observer, nothing else is needed.
8. Now follow a thought from the time it arises to the time it fades away. Through your observing, can you find the place from where thoughts arise? This question is not to be thought about; its answer needs to be observed and experienced by you.
9. Where do thoughts go when they disappear from awareness? Can you observe this?
10. Notice that after a thought fades, and before the next thought appears, there is a space or emptiness. Place your attention on this space. Do not exert any effort in this observing; do not try to locate this space. Simply allow

yourself to be the observer. This space will come into your awareness when you allow the mind's phenomena to come and go on their own accord, without any interference from you.
11. Can you know a thought before it appears in your awareness?
12. If you can observe your thoughts, can you be your thoughts?

This meditation takes practice before you clearly perceive the arising and fading of thought. If you can experience this silent space, know that this space is also perceived by you. Where does this silent space arise from? From the Buddhist perspective, it arises from Ku, just like everything else.

With a better understanding of Ku, we can now discuss non-substantiality. From a dualistic perspective, we see ourselves, and everything around us, as being a separate entity unto itself and with a fixed nature. I see myself as a separate entity from my dog. I also see both my dog and me as being of a fixed nature. I will always be me, and my dog will always be a dog.

From the perspective of non-substantiality, the essence of who I am is not me. Similarly, the essence of my dog is not a dog. Both my dog and I are the manifested expressions of Ku. Instead of being fixed, both my dog and I are dynamic beings that are undergoing constant change at all levels of our being. Further, both my dog and I have the potential for unlimited change. What does separate me from my dog is that I have the self-awareness that allows me to consciously express that unlimited potential for change. The benefit of mastering the mind is the ability to harness that potential.

Since everything is an expression of Ku, the conscious changes that I make in my life can create positive changes for everything in my environment. In other words, life is fluid, dynamic, and constantly changing. Nothing in life is fixed or stays the same. No matter what challenges we face, we have the potential to change so that we can meet that challenge. It is when we adopt disempowering beliefs such as "this always happens to me," or "my life will never change," that we feel stuck in life. You, the people in your life, and the situations that you experience are fluid and constantly changing. You will realize this if you can move beyond the illusions that are created by the mind.

# Chapter Ten

# One's Life and the Environment

*"Irrigators channel waters; fletchers straighten arrows; carpenters shape wood; the wise master themselves."*

—The Buddha

The principles of non-substantiality and non-duality provide us with a context for the principle of the oneness of our life and the environment. In Western culture's dualistic perspective, we see our lives as being separate from the environment. It is this perspective that leads us to carry out violence toward others as well as ecological destruction. War, repression, prejudice, and aggression are all ways that we dehumanize others because we see them as being less than ourselves. As for the Earth, we clear rainforests, burn fossil fuel, pollute the oceans and streams, and cause species to become endangered or extinct. We do this because we believe the purpose of the Earth is to fulfill our needs. More importantly, we do it because we see the Earth as being separate from ourselves.

In Buddhism, our lives and the environment are inseparable from each other. The principle of non-substantiality points to the fact that we are not distinct entities, nor are our lives static. There is nothing that is inherently you, nor is your environment inherently it. Your neighborhood is not inherently a neighborhood. Your city or state is not inherently a city or state. Instead, you, your neighborhood, your city, and your state are dynamic expressions of Ku. At the level of Ku, everything is one. Because everything is inherently one, our karma interacts with the environment, and our environment interacts with us. Here is an example:

A person's life is based on fear. This person fears that they will never be happy unless the conditions of their life are met. One condition that they believe they need to be happy is to be rich. To get rich, they build a factory to produce a product. Because their goal is to be rich, they neglect to observe environmental regulations, thus polluting the water and air.

This person pursues money, which is born out of desire. Their desire is born from memory, a memory based on fear. Their fear is based on a belief that they need to pursue something outside themselves to achieve happiness, which in this case is money. The polluting of the environment is the action that they engage in based on the desire for money.

As a result of the polluted environment, this person develops cancer. Because the environment became unhealthy, so did the person. Both the person and his environment are one; they share the same karma. The environment is the mirror of the person's inner life, as they are both unhealthy. If this person changes their karma, their environment will also change.

Our experience of unhappiness is not the result of our environment, though that is what we focus on when we are unhappy. How we experience our environment is dependent on the conditions of our inner world. The environment is just a mirror of our inner lives. We need to change our inner lives before we can change the environment. Everything that we experience originates from within us. The relationship between us and our environment is both dynamic and inseparable. Whatever changes we make within ourselves will be reflected in our environment. Buddhism teaches how to release our infinite potential as a human being so that we can create positive change in the world around us.

# Chapter Eleven

# Sentient and Non-Sentient Beings

*"In whom there is no sympathy for living beings: know him as an outcast."*

—The Buddha

Buddhism refers to living and non-living beings as being sentient or non-sentient. A being that has the five components (aggregates) is considered sentient, while a being that does not have the five aggregates is considered non-sentient. The five components are form, perception, conception, volition, and consciousness.

- Form refers to the physical aspects of life, including the five senses and the physical body, which are used to perceive the world.
- Perception is the function of collecting information from the external world through the six sense organs (the mind is considered the sixth sense organ). Perception integrates the information from the external world.
- Conception is the process of converting the integrated information from the six senses and creating a mental image of it.

- Volition is the will to act upon the mental image created by conception as well as the motivation of action.
- Consciousness discerns and integrates the previous four components.

From a Buddhist perspective, it is unethical to inflict suffering on a sentient being. To cause suffering in others is a source of bad karma. As the goal of Buddhism is to purify the mind, the development of compassion is fundamental. In Buddhism, nothing is more sacred than the gift of life.

## Chapter Twelve

# Attachment

*"A mind unruffled by the vagaries of fortune, from sorrow freed, from defilements cleansed, from fear liberated—this is the greatest blessing."*

—The Buddha

Imagine that you are walking alone down an empty street at night in the bad area of town. As you are walking, you hear the sound of footsteps behind you. Suddenly you feel fearful, wondering what you should do. Your whole body becomes tense, and your mind is imaging what this person may do to you. Every aspect of your being is feeling a sense of terror.

Now imagine that you are watching a movie and a scene appears where the main character is walking down an empty street at night, just as in the first scenario. You feel yourself getting emotionally involved as you anticipate what may happen to the main character. Though you are fully engaged with what is happening in the scene, a part of you realizes that it is just a movie. You can experience this suspenseful moment while enjoying the experience. You can enjoy this experience because you are, at some level detached, from the experience.

Another important core principle of Buddhism is detachment from the functions of the mind and body. Through the process of mindfulness practices, including meditation, we can learn to experience all of life without becoming attached to any of it. Increased awareness through meditation leads to the realization that who we are is not the functions of the mind and body. Our essential self is the one who is aware of the mind and body functions. When we lack this awareness, then our sense of wellbeing becomes dictated by our environment. The following is an example:

Janet wakes up early in the morning for her daily jog before she goes to work. As she is running, she has a feeling of peace from experiencing the beauty and calm of the morning. But her sense of peace is short-lived as she stumbles and sprains her ankle. Now, Janet is feeling upset and frustrated because she is in pain.

As a result of the accident, she finds herself running late for work. While driving to work, she is worried because she has an important meeting to attend. She calls work to advise her manager that she will be late. Her manager tells her not to worry as the meeting was canceled. Now Janet experiences a sense of relief.

Janet arrives at work and is advised that her manager wants to speak to her. She feels worry. When Janet meets with her manager, however, she tells her that she will be receiving a promotion. Now, Janet is feeling excited and happy. At the end of the day, Janet drives home but winds up in a minor traffic accident; a car rear ends her new vehicle. Janet is irate.

This scenario of Janet's day demonstrates how our state of being is constantly changing based on the situations and events that we experience. In the course of one day, Janet went from relaxed, calm, upset, frustrated, anxious, relieved, worried, excited, happy, and irate. There is nothing wrong with experiencing these emotions; our emotions are what makes us human. Our problems occur when we allow our thoughts and emotions to determine our state of wellbeing or our sense of identity.

Most of us are like Janet as we allow the ever-changing circumstances of our lives to determine how we feel about ourselves. The reason why our circumstances affect how we feel about ourselves is that we have allowed our circumstances to shape our sense of identity.

From a very young age, we learned that to get our needs met, we needed to win the approval of others. As infants, we learned that we are dependent on our parents for comfort, nourishment, and security. As we got older, we learned that we needed to conform to our parents' expectations if we wanted their approval. The seeking of approval continued as we advanced through life. We sought the approval of friends, teachers, employers, and society as a whole.

If I believe my success is dependent upon me being good at my job, doing well in school, and having a good relationship with my partner, then I will strive for these things so that I can feel good about myself. Let us say that I am successful in attaining all of these goals. Having accomplished these things, I feel happy and successful. But, how long will that happiness last? What if I get laid off my job? What happens if my grades drop or my partner leaves me?

When our sense of identity is based on external conditions, our sense of wellbeing will be dependent on our circumstances meeting our expectations. Given that the phenomenal world is in constant flux, we will never experience a lasting sense of peace and happiness. It is only when we establish our sense self in that which does not change that we can enjoy true peace and happiness. When we reach this state, it is referred to as enlightenment. Enlightenment is the mastering of the mind.

The following exercise will guide you toward reducing your attachments. By increasing your awareness to the impermanence of the phenomenal world, which includes everything that we experience, your attachments will naturally lose their potency.

# Exercise #6

1. Sit down and make yourself comfortable. Allow yourself to become relaxed.
2. Now observe something. It can be anything—an object, a person, your own body, or nature.
3. As you observe your subject, ask yourself if there anything about this object that is impermanent, that is subject to change? Can you find anything about this object that could change over time?

4. If your answer is "No," then look more deeply. Nothing that we can experience through our thoughts or five senses is free from change.

When working with attachment, it can be helpful to go back and repeat Exercise #1, practicing to observe and finding the one who is observing. If you have trouble finding the observer, do not become frustrated. Your failure to find the observer means that you are on the right track. The observer is non-phenomenal as well as being the truth of who you are.

The amount of attachment that we have in our lives determines our life condition. Those who have strong attachment to the mind and body have a low life condition. Those who lose their attachment to the mind and body reveal their enlightened nature. The Nichiren school of Buddhism has a practical model to determine our state of life, which is referred to as the Ten Worlds.

## Chapter Thirteen

# The Ten Worlds

*"Whoever doesn't flare up at someone who's angry wins a battle hard to win."*

—The Buddha

The Ten Worlds is a model in Buddhist philosophy that depicts the various life states that a person can occupy. The Ten Worlds are as follows: Hell, Anger, Hunger, Animality, Heaven, Humanity, Learning, Realization, Bodhisattva, and Buddhahood. These worlds are not outside us; they represent the states of our life force. Hell is the lowest state while Buddhahood is the highest. The following is a description of each of these worlds:

Hell. Hell is the lowest life state a human can occupy. This tenth world is characterized by the feeling that we are the targets of life's misfortunes and that we are powerless to change our situation. This is the state of life that leads some people to become addicted to smoking, alcohol, drugs, spending money, or committing suicide. When in Hell, we see no hope for a better future.

Anger. Anger is characterized by the need to dominate others or having an uncontrolled competitive desire to surpass others. Anger is the second lowest state. The world of Anger can lead us to take action, rather than giving in to the helpless feeling that is associated with the world of Hell.

**Animality.** Animality is the eighth world and is characterized by the state of life where a person exhibits animal-like qualities in the way that they interact with other people. They dominate or intimidate those that they see as being weaker than themselves but try to appease those that they view as being more powerful. The world of Animality reflects the popular concept of the "law of the jungle," where the mighty prey on the weak. Examples of this world can be found everywhere, from the schoolyard bully to the Wall Street shark.

**Hunger.** Hunger is the seventh world and is characterized by someone who has an insatiable desire that can never be fulfilled. Whether it is relationships, money, power, or approval, this person is relentless in their pursuit of that which they desire. This desire is just an illusion. If a person in the world of Hunger manages to obtain that which they want, they will be satisfied only momentarily. This person will have a brief period of satisfaction before experiencing a need to meet the next desire. Examples of this world would be people who are addicted to relationships, alcohol, drugs, power, prestige, or attention.

**Humanity.** The world of humanity is the sixth world and is characterized by the state of life characterized by calm thinking and sound judgment.

**Rapture.** The world of Rapture is characterized by a sense of joy that is associated with fulfilling a desire or overcoming a great suffering.

The previous six worlds (Hell, Anger, Animality, Hunger, Humanity, and Rapture) are referred to as the lower worlds because they are unstable. They arise within us as a result of changes in the conditions of our surrounding. For example, the person who is in the world of Animality will be dutiful when his manager speaks to him but may yell at his secretary when he or she makes a mistake. Such a person's sense of identity is not stable but is determined by who they are interacting with. Similarly, a person can be in the world of Rapture because they have come into the possession of a large amount of money. If they are unwise in how they manage their money, they could lose it all and drop into the world of Anger or Hell. Because the lower worlds are impermanent and constantly changing, they lead to a sense of uncertainty, doubt, fear, or anxiousness. The next four worlds are referred to as the higher worlds.

**Learning.** The seventh world, the world of learning, involves developing a desire to understand the deeper meaning of life and to expand in awareness. We find ourselves wanting to discover the truth about ourselves and the nature of who we are. This is the fundamental role of ethics, religion, and spirituality, which is to get us to stop focusing so much on the physical world and more on our inner world.

**Realization.** The world of Realization is the eighth world and is similar to the world of Learning with one exception. Instead of relying on outside sources of inspiration for discovering our truth, we develop an awareness in which the answers to our questions become self-evident. In other words, we find our answers by going within.

**Bodhisattva.** The ninth world, the world of the Bodhisattva, is when we dedicate our lives to becoming enlightened. But this dedication to seeking enlightenment must be connected with working for the happiness of others. It is through the working for the happiness of others that the ego is subordinated and our enlightened nature is revealed.

These last three worlds (Learning, Realization, and Bodhisattva) are considered the higher worlds. At these levels, we grow increasingly less reactive to our environment. Rather than reacting, we respond to life with wisdom, compassion, and courage. Instead of basing our sense of self on the situations and events of our lives, our sense of being is anchored in our enlightened nature, also known as the Buddha nature.

The tenth world is that of **Buddhahood**. This world is very difficult to explain in words as it exists beyond our conceptual understanding. The world of Buddhahood can be best described through the qualities of ultimate freedom, equanimity, and boundless wisdom. In the world of Buddhahood, all sense of separateness, limitation, and suffering dissolve. When a person achieves Buddhahood, they have the freedom of transcending the conceptual mind while enjoying the world of experience.

The Ten Worlds are mutually inclusive of each other, meaning that each world contains the remaining nine worlds within it. This means that regardless of the world we are in, the world of Buddhahood lies within us. It also means that the world of Buddhahood has the other nine worlds in it, including the lowest world, Hell. These lower worlds, however, change how they function when in the world of Buddhahood. The lower worlds function in a manner that supports us in our happiness. They exhibit their noble qualities to enhance our lives. Without the wisdom of enlightenment, the lower worlds are experienced in their illusionary state, which leads to suffering.

Throughout the day, we shift from world to world. But each of us has a baseline world, the world in which we spend most of our time. The following exercise will allow you to track the worlds that you experience as you go through your day. With this awareness, you can use the exercises in this book to reach higher worlds.

# Exercise #8

1. Review the section on the Ten Worlds and become familiar with them.
2. Throughout the day, take a moment and observe your emotions and state of being.
3. Based on your observations, try to identify which of the Ten Worlds you are experiencing.
4. At the end of the day, identify which of the Ten Worlds you spent most time in.
5. This kind of introspection will allow you to understand your current state of life. You can then ask yourself which worlds you would like to experience more often.

6. When you have decided on the world that you would like to experience more often, ask yourself what you would need to believe to make that possible.
7. Condition your mind to adopt this belief by focusing on all the positive outcomes you would receive by making this new belief your reality. Conversely, think of all the negatives you would experience if you do not change your existing belief.
8. Whenever you find yourself demonstrating your new belief, through your actions, find a way to reward yourself at that moment, even if it is simply telling yourself "Good job!" You can follow-up later by rewarding yourself in a manner that you find more meaningful.

# Conclusion

In the introduction of this book, you read the parable of the *Jewel in the Robe*. The takeaway from that parable is that we experience suffering because we are unaware of our true nature, which is unbounded potential. It is only the mind that creates our experience of limitations.

Ultimately, every one of us has one desire: to be happy. But even the pursuit of happiness is an illusion. Happiness is an emotional state that comes and goes like all other emotions. Ultimate success in life is to transcend the conditioning of the mind and to experience life with greater clarity. When we do this, we will experience a level of peace and connection with life that is beyond our ordinary experience. To say this peace and connection is beyond our ordinary experience is not to say that practicing Buddhism makes us extraordinary. Rather, what we consider to be extraordinary is actually our natural state of being.

The purpose of Buddhism is to guide us back to what makes us essentially human, which is beyond our ordinary experience. Humanity is going through numerous challenges as we face everything from environmental destruction to nuclear war. It should be clear by now that government, policies, regulations, and laws have not been effective in protecting us from these and other existential threats. Only when each of us takes time to see ourselves and others more clearly can we gain the momentum to change the direction of human history. Buddhism offers the tools for doing so.

Printed in Poland
by Amazon Fulfillment
Poland Sp. z o.o., Wrocław